A GUIDE TO OUTREACH WITH LAPTOPS

Angela Wood

Published by the National Institute of
Adult Continuing Education (England and Wales)

21 De Montfort Street
Leicester LE1 7GE
Company registration no. 2603322
Charity registration no. 1002775

First published 2000
Reprinted 2001

NIACE, the national organisation for adult learning, has a broad remit to promote lifelong learning opportunities for adults. NIACE works to develop increased participation in education and trainging, particularly for those who do not have easy access because of barriers of class, gender, age, race, language and culture, learning difficulties and disabilities, or insufficient financial resources.

NIACE's website on the Internet is:
http://www.niace.org.uk

Cataloguing in Publication Data
A CIP record of this title is available from the British Library

Typeset by Avon DataSet Ltd, Bidford on Avon,
Warwickshire B50 4JH (www.avondataset.com)

Printed in Great Britain by Alden Press

ISBN: 1 86201 109 5

Contents

Credits

This guide would not have been possible without all the contributions from the people working out there, doing it!

Focus group: Roger Drury, Community Media Worker, Forest of Dean; Mary Turner Outreach Worker, Exeter College; Claire Mycock, Training and Development Co-ordinator, Northampton Lifelong Learning Service; Anita McGreal, Adult Education Officer, Training Department, Leeds City Council; Robert Whittaker, Community Project Officer, Groundwork, Leeds; Anne Sturzaker, ICT Development Officer, Lancashire County Council; Brian Chadwick, Community Development Project Officer, Adult and Community Education Service, Wakefield; Keith Rooney, Family Learning Officer, St Helens; Kathy Seacome, Development Worker, Barnsley Metropolitan Borough Council Community Resources; Patsy Cummings, Acting Manager, CALTEC (Bradford LEA); Alan Dyer, Tutor, Leeds City Council; Marilyn Spencer, High Wycombe YMCA.

Network: Forty two people attended four workshops at two network events.

Mailgroup: Lorraine Tuckey, Milton Keynes; Gordon Anderson, Devon County Council; John Carley, Project One O One; Bola Odepidan, African and Caribbean Project; Mercy Addo, Wandsworth; Maurice Neville, Derbyshire LEA Adult Community Education Service; Dr G Trodd, London Borough of Harrow; Christine Clifford; Harry Fairtlough, Buckinghamshire; Tania Scott; Neil Towell, Warrington College Institute, Ian McGregor, Derbyshire County Council.

Contributions from: Annie Merton, Development Officer, NIACE; Veronica McGivney, Development Officer, NIACE; Alistair Thomson, Development Officer, NIACE; Rosemary Napper, Personal and Professional Development Officer, Oxfordshire County Council; Fiona Aldridge, Research Officer and Alan Clarke ICT Development Officer, NIACE.

Many thanks to Patsy Cummings, CALTEC, Bradford, Anita McGreal, Leeds and Oxfordshire County Council Adult Education Service for allowing us to incorporate examples of the paperwork they have developed for use with the laptops.

I would like to thank the Department for Education and Employment who provided the funding for this work and the laptop project as a whole.

I would also like to thank Alan Clarke for allowing me to reproduce the 'Laptop Buyers Guide'

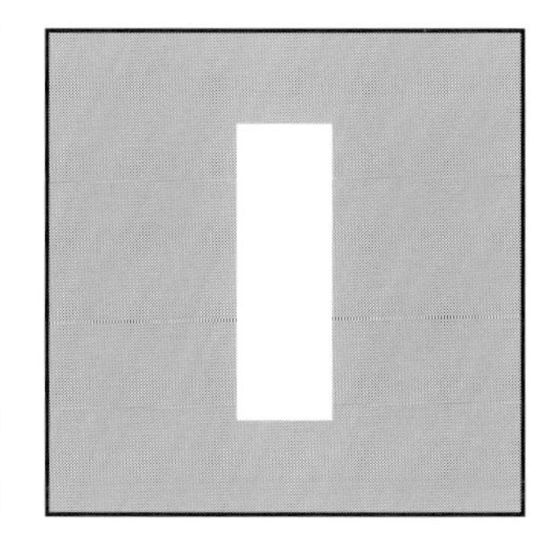

Introduction

There is no denying the impact that technology is having on the world around us; nor for that matter on adult and community learning. When the Department for Education and Employment decided to commit £4m to 'The Laptop Initiative for Adult and Community Learning' they anticipated that they would influence the use of technology amongst tutors and organisations. The range and scale of this influence has been dramatic.

For many organisations this initiative was the first time they had worked in adult and community learning with laptops and ICT equipment; for others this resource was an addition to ageing equipment.

This guide focuses on how the laptops are and could be used innovatively, creatively and resourcefully in Basic Skills, Outreach and Widening Participation generally.

Within the guide there are examples of models of delivery examining what worked and, in some cases, what didn't work. There is a chapter devoted to best practice in developing a laptop-based project. You will also find contained within this guide practical methods of outreach work with the laptops and philosophical discussion around strategies and skills of outreach.

This guide is intended for:

- Outreach workers;
- Community Development workers;
- Tutors;
- Managers; and
- Co-ordinators.

DFEE LAPTOP INITIATIVE

Aims of the Initiative

The aim of the initiative is to develop innovative applications of laptops in:

- basic skills education
- community outreach
- pursuit of the widening participation agenda generally.

The laptops have been given to organisations in order to:

- enrich teaching
- provide quality support for learners
- see ICT as a regular feature in literacy and other provision.

Management of the Initiative

The Laptop Initiative for Adult and Community Learning is managed for the Department for Education and Employment by two prominent organisations in the field of adult learning, the National Institute of Adult Continuing Education (NIACE) and the Basic Skills Agency (BSA).

Through this initiative, the DfEE has loaned 1500 laptop packages to approximately 300 LEAs and voluntary and community organisations in England.

For further information on the initiative please contact:

Alan Clarke or Fiona Aldridge at NIACE on 0116 204 4200 or by email at alanc@niace.org.uk or fiona@niace.org.uk

Andrea Mearing at BSA on 0171 405 4017

Dissemination of good practice

Case studies submitted by many projects involved with this initiative have been posted on the NIACE website:

http://www.niace.org.uk/Research/ICT/laptops/goodpractice.htm

How this Guide was produced

The laptop initiative provided resources to capture the experience of participants. This guide is part of the process of capturing good practice. Angela Wood, Outreach Co-ordinator with Oxfordshire

County Council, agreed to develop this outreach guide. Outreach is an essential feature of adult and community learning which has been sadly underdeveloped in recent years.

The development process included:
- laptop networking events;
- a discussion paper produced and distributed via the mailgroup;
- mailgroup discussions; and
- focus groups.

If you wish to subscribe to the mailgroup, please send an e-mail to Listcaster@niace.org.uk with the following message:

Subscribe Making-IT-Accessible

Principles of outreach

It would seem that recent developments in adult and community learning are putting outreach back on the agenda.

Little has been written about outreach in the last ten years, a period during which there has been a significant loss of LEA funding for community education. Outreach has been significantly reduced as an indirect result of the 1992 Further and Higher Education Act and the funding and organisational changes it introduced. Helena Kennedy QC, in her report *Learning Works*, identified Further Education Funding Council funding methodology as unintentionally operating as a disincentive to outreach. Both colleges and local authorities found it hard to fund outreach when it was easier to secure funding by encouraging 'safer' students, i.e. easier to accommodate students who need less development and support to get started.

Initiatives such as the DfEE-funded laptop initiative would seem to be offering a way of reversing the trend and nurturing bottom-up community development.

During 1997 and 1998 the DfEE funded 12 demonstration outreach projects, the overall aim being to develop innovative ways of improving access to information and advice on learning opportunities in disadvantaged communities. A final report and six briefings are available on the website at www.lifelonglearning.co.uk/outreach

WHY OUTREACH?

How would *you* answer this question?

- Because it is central to the widening participation agenda?
- To attract people who would not normally use a service and do not realise what is on offer?
- Picking up where the marketing team has 'failed'?

What is your purpose for undertaking outreach work?

- Are you outreaching to bring people into your planned provision?

- Is it to develop relevant methods of educational delivery?
- Are you wishing to become more aware of the community needs and concerns?
- Do you want to identify new groups who have educational needs that are not being met?

The fundamental principle of outreach development work is starting from where the people are.

- Are you taking a service to people who would not otherwise access your provision because of difficulties with transport and location?
- Within the community, are you focusing on 'target' groups?

What is meant by 'outreach'?

It is difficult to give one definition of outreach as in recent years when the term 'outreach' has been used it has meant the following:

- A provider making off-site provision;
- A central body (College, LEA, etc.) reaching out to its periphery to bring people in;
- Larger providers working with or through smaller local providers.

DO WE NEED ANOTHER TERM FOR OUTREACH WHEN WE USE THE SAME WORD WITH A COMMUNITY DEVELOPMENT MODEL?

Outreach work within a community development model goes further than this. It has closer links to community education of the 1970s and can be traced back to the efforts of the universities from the late nineteenth century to extend a university culture to a wider population through extra-mural classes and university settlements in the East End. It is used in this sense in a book called *Learning Networks in Adult Education* (Fordham *et al*, 1979), where outreach tutors are also referred to as 'community workers', 'facilitators' and 'animateurs' and outreach work is seen as:

> "developing non-formal work in a neighbourhood . . . so programmes can become more closely related to the expectations and wishes of local people"

A definition of outreach offered in 1986 (Ward, 1986) was:

> "Outreach is a process whereby people who would not normally use adult education are contacted in non-institutional settings and become involved in attending and eventually in jointly planning and controlling activities, schemes and courses relevant to their circumstances and needs"

Is this definition still relevant in 2000?

> 'In an ideal world this would be a perfect definition. In reality I spend so much of my time trying to contact people that often the definition stops there. I would change the order of the last part of the definition as effective outreach brings in joint planning at the start before people begin to attend.' (Milton Keynes)

What is outreach?

The rich response of laptop participants is reproduced here in their own words.

- Outreach is just a new word for working in the community.
- Outreach is essentially about convincing people, who may have originally rejected education as a means of improving their learning, into declaring their learning needs and negotiating what and how they would like to learn.
- It means the process by which you will go out and actively engage people. Many people are trapped (in quite a small geographical area, by childcare responsibilities). So you have to go out to them in the form of a person, speak to them and attract them to whatever it is you have to offer.
- It is about consultation, finding out what community groups want and what people want. There are different ways of doing that like roadshows.
- It's about widening participation and for it to be effective, you could go out there and promote your centre, promote your course, but you're far better putting on courses in places that people are familiar with.
- It's about evaluating what already exists, rather than trying to reinvent the wheel. Because there is a community out there, there's a lot of research needed in identifying the key leaders and getting them involved. It takes time to identify community groups and individuals. Take advantage of people that are already involved, maintain involvement with them; that is more likely to succeed than dropping leaflets in the post and just going away and hoping. That simply doesn't work.
- Outreach is building bridges. Enabling people within communities to access educational provision. It can be years and years before they are ready to move out of those communities into somewhere else, or even to the community that's a mile down the road. We've had people say: 'We're not going there, we're not going into a class with that lot'.

You talk to the two different communities, and one lot say, 'they're a bit snobby', and the other lot say 'they're a bit rough there' and there is only half a mile separating them.

- Outreach is building bridges between the communities. It is all sorts. I think there's a responsiveness that outreach gives, because it doesn't necessarily work on terms, or anything like that, in a way that you can't with physical infrastructure, so I like the responsiveness. There's also – it's the familiar environment, the comfortable environment which is not perceived as a learning environment, working men's clubs, pubs, it's fine to use them as a learning situation, 'so let's have a beer break', things that you can never do in a classroom situation.
- Outreach means looking for opportunities. Not just going with what you've got already, but looking for new alternatives. You've just got to keep your eyes open and look for places to take your laptops to.
- The fascinating thing about outreach work is that you might have some success, with a disadvantaged estate, you develop a model of working and it's been great but a big mistake is to assume that model will work in another area with the exact same characteristics.
- You've got to be imaginative, respond to circumstances as they emerge; they're always different; that's what I find very interesting about outreach; you're learning all the time. You develop models which you think would fit into a certain area, then you try it and discover something else. There is no perfect model.
- Education by stealth.
- It's a very gradual process and there has to be ways of applauding the smallest victory.
- When you are outreaching with the purpose of recruitment, to attract people onto courses, it is very irritating to be confined to funding rules. When you are actually doing outreach work you are engaged in community development.
- A lot of outreach work involves information giving and information gathering, being able to refer people to other services.
- Outreach takes time and you have to build from the bottom.
- Outreach is a way of building partnerships so that our service can be extended to other groups that we couldn't reach in any other way. Laptops are a good way of taking our computer provision we

have in our centre to environments where people feel comfortable and empowering them to do whatever they want. Helping people to move on in their lives and not necessarily getting anywhere near moving them into formal education provision; we're talking a long way back along the line.

- Outreach with the laptops offers a new dimension to outreach. Using laptops, there is a portable electronic world to offer to communities.
- Outreach is about motivation and motivation comes from self-respect. How do you quantify gains in self-respect? How quickly can such gains be achieved?

OUTREACH IS . . .

If as a learning organisation you want to work in the community to develop learning opportunities, then having considered '***Why?***', your next question will be '***How?***' Below is a table with stages of outreach and models you may wish to consider. This is explored further in the next two chapters.

Where does your Outreach Work fit into this model?

Purpose	Method	Practicalities	Resources
• Making contacts	Hands-on session	• Will need to show people very basic skills, e.g. how to use a mouse	• Trolley to transport laptops
• Engaging with local people	Taster sessions	• Use volunteers or staffing ration of two people to one laptop	• Plenty of CD ROMS for fun: IT for ALL, Webwise, In-House, etc.
• Individual development	One to One	• Confidence building for writing CVs, job search skills, accessing Internet	• Websites for accessing internet
		• May identify basic skills needs and be in a position to offer referrals or training to meet needs	• Guidance programmes, e.g. Adult Directions
• Group development and exploration	Short courses	• Sessions lasting one and a half to two hours offered in a venue identified by local people: (e.g. pubs and sheltered housing)	• Tutors need to be experienced in ICT and to be flexible and adaptable about working with community groups' needs
		• May identify further training needs so you will need to have a clear idea of progression opportunities	
• Specific target groups	Small groups	• Project work, e.g. Tenants, Residents, Homestart	

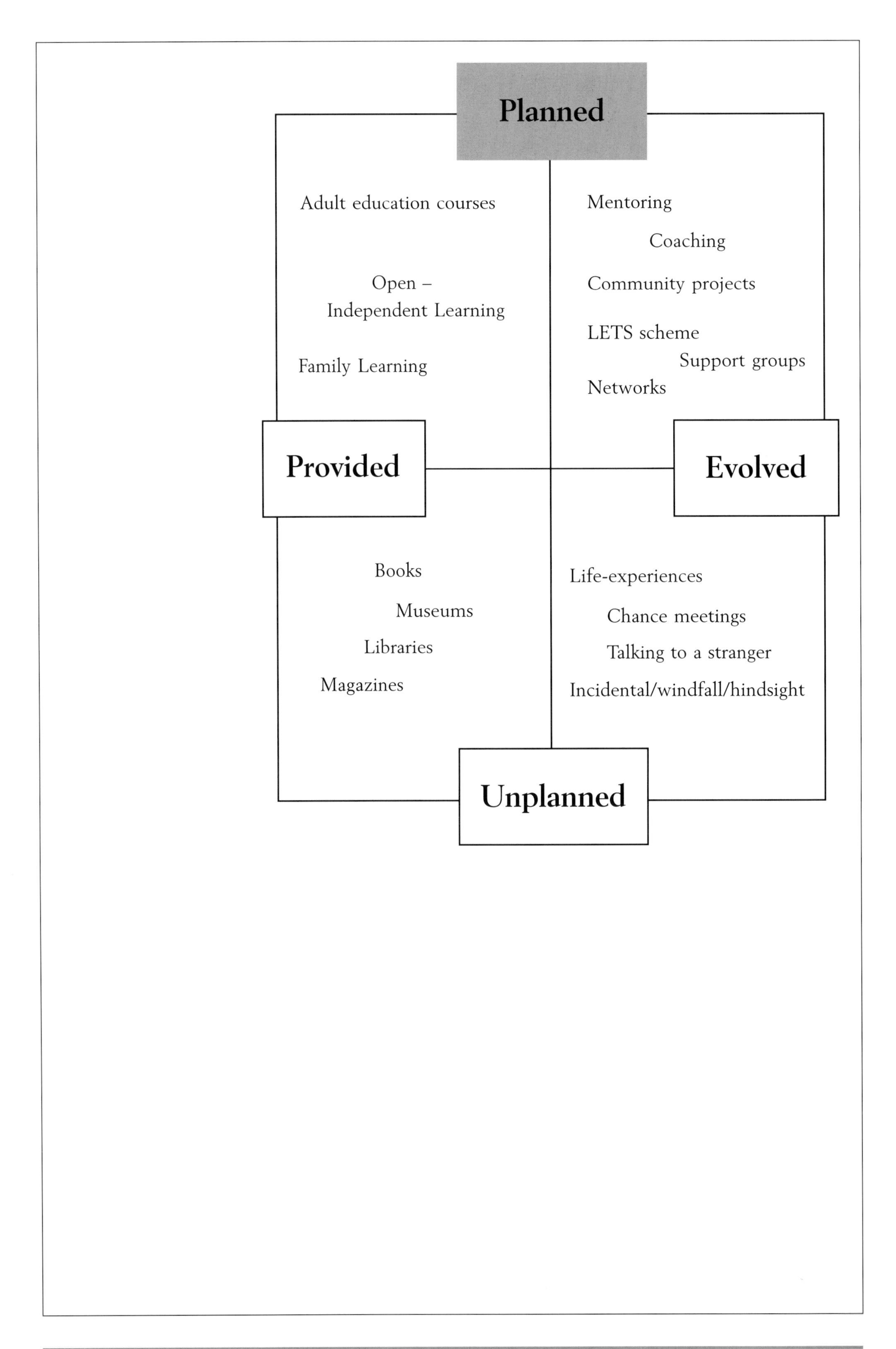
Planned
Adult education courses
Open –
Independent Learning
Family Learning
Mentoring
Coaching
Community projects
LETS scheme
Support groups
Networks
Provided
Evolved
Books
Museums
Libraries
Magazines
Life-experiences
Chance meetings
Talking to a stranger
Incidental/windfall/hindsight
Unplanned

Models of delivery

What may work in one area, at one time and with one group, may not work again in a different area with a similar group. Therefore it is important to have a wide range of strategies, knowledge and understanding of different models. It may be that you are working on short-term funding and are only concerned with one project. Or you may already be doing outreach in a community and the following examples of strategies and models of delivery will give you some ideas on how to further develop community ICT learning.

The number of laptops available may determine the model you use.

Any piece of work has a series of phases:

The Initial Phase:	when we ask why we want to do something, what we want to achieve, what resources are needed and who will be involved
The Start up Phase:	when we ask how we will go about the work, when we are going to do it and whether it is feasible
The Development Phase:	when we get on with the work
The Evaluation Phase:	when we ask what happened and how and what we have learned from it
The Dissemination Phase:	when we share what we have learnt with others.

LEARNING TO LEARN

For many adults, information technology is associated with a lack of confidence and uncertainty. Adults who overcome their doubts to take part in an initial event need an experience that encourages them to want more. It is quite possible within a short period to provide an experience which starts to develop confidence and encourages them to return.

A useful and informative guide by Clarke (1999) has been written with the aim of providing a straightforward summary of good practice based on NIACE projects and research. It is aimed at ICT tutors and their managers who are undertaking or planning a learning programme. It is equally relevant to outreach and development workers.

It covers the initial event and subsequent sessions including working on an outreach basis. The emphasis is on developing confidence and providing a sound initial learning programme, which will provide a foundation for further study. It covers planning and undertaking different types of events as well as teaching techniques and advice on how to achieve successful sessions. It is well worth a read!

DEVELOPING CONFIDENT LEARNERS

A whole range of models is available to develop outreach work with Information and Communication Technology learning opportunities. What follows are summaries and examples of some of the many ways organisations are working to successfully encourage adults to learn and become competent users of ICT.

Supporting existing provision

The laptops have proved valuable with existing community and basic skills provision. Recipients of the DfEE laptops report an increase in recruitment to basic skills groups since using laptops.

Examples of how the laptops are used include:

- An existing Wordpower group had the use of laptops. People attending the group spread the word that there were laptops and recruitment grew. As a result, additional basic skills classes have been provided.
- Basic Skills Summer Schools used them to offer Open College Network-accredited Basic Skills through computer courses.
- Family Numeracy projects are able to use the laptops for sessions. This has given students access to learning numeracy skills whilst learning some basics of computers.
- Family Literacy projects have used the laptops to develop literacy skills in the production of story sacks and book making.
- Family Learning Weekend in conjunction with literacy initiative 'Read on – Write Away'
- 'The Knowledge' – a course equipping ESOL and EAL taxi drivers to take the knowledge test to apply for a Hackney licence.

Loaned to groups

When laptops are loaned out to groups they are used to reach out to potential new learners. The focus is more on providing informal learning opportunities.

- St Helen's Adult Education Service allocated three community centres a laptop each. The centre managers then co-ordinated their use for groups who are using the centre: mothers and toddlers, badminton groups, historical societies, etc.
- Derbyshire loaned a scanner and printer to a Millennium writing project on an isolated estate.
- In Exeter, a community association group used the laptop to produce a calendar; this was then sold at Christmas to raise funds. They printed and laminated the calendars as and when people wanted them.
- An 'Older and Bolder' group have used the laptops for an *Introduction to Computers* course.
- A pilot scheme targeting African and Caribbean women who are over 50 and have no IT knowledge. The scheme has been offering free IT short courses to two/three women in their homes.

"The way we have used the laptops is not so much to deliver courses but to use them to reach out to potential new learners. They are loaned to groups – small, interest, service groups – with some basic software as an outreach post of our 'IT for ALL' initiative. Tutor/facilitator hours are allocated with an option to 'but-in' expertise from a local provider. The aim is to enable target/membership or interest groups to have access to a laptop to explore, identify questions and use when it suits them and then have someone to help with problems. This way of working provides people with basic introduction, interest and the confidence to move into a course."

(Wandsworth)

Co-ordinated projects

LEEDS CITY COUNCIL ADULT EDUCATION co-ordinates the laptops from one central base. The co-ordination is within an existing manager's time. Co-ordination means employing technicians and tutors, and organising where the laptops go. Allocation is according to two different models: either an accredited course or an LEA-funded course. In order to make allocation easier, a computer diary planner is used.

'Computers on Wheels' has developed as a project using two sets of laptops, scanners, internet access, digital camera and up-to-date software. Community groups are invited to request the service. The criteria for use of the service is as follows:

- Participants must be over 16 and be one of the City Council's priority groups
- Venues must satisfy health and safety requirements and be secure
- Sessions must be in the daytime and have a maximum of eight attending
- Priority will be given to inner city venues with no other IT resource
- Adequate progression routes and guidance should be available for students after the course
- Programmes will run for a maximum of one term with any specific group
- Priority will be given to providing accredited provision for unemployed adults.

Courses on offer:

- Family Literacy support sessions (book-making and story writing)
- Open College accreditation (up to Level 2 in Word Processing, Spreadsheet, and Database)
- Newsletter groups and Desktop Publishing courses
- Group guidance sessions (for Family Literacy courses only) using Adult Directions software.
- The key to the success of the project is that technicians accompany each session. They pick up the computers from the base, take them to the groups, set them up, remain with the group throughout the session (this also offers additional security) and then return the computers to the base or go onto the next session. A flatbed trolley saves the technicians from too much lifting.
- In a one-term period the laptops have been used to support fourteen groups. A further 15 one-off sessions have been offered. The project has been widened following demand for training in computer maintenance and installation. Using 'rescued' PCs, a number of courses have been established. Having stimulated demand with the laptops it has been possible to equip two neighbourhood centres with stand-alone machines.

DERBYSHIRE ADULT COMMUNITY EDUCATION SERVICE was allocated 16 laptops, printers and scanners. A decision was made to divide the set into two (eight laptops, four printers and scanner) and allocate within the County to two specific areas. This then left eight printers and scanners to be used in other areas to involve the rest of the county in the project.

- Both sets are stored in secure main centres and are then available to be used anywhere in the district. This simplified transportation requirements.

- An important outcome of the laptop initiative is the involvement with the District Community Learning Partnership promoting inter-agency widening participation work at grassroots level. A working group has been set up to use the laptops for capacity-building and access to learning. This involves Community Service Volunteers, Social Services Day Care Services and Community Education. Voluntary groups in the district will be given ICT training which they will then cascade to their clients. The Learning Partnership is funding the training.

NORTH NOTTINGHAMSHIRE COLLEGE has concentrated the use of the laptops in the rural ex-mining communities. These communities are isolated and for those without transport, access to large towns is difficult. Mobile ICT workshops using the laptops have been set up in many of the communities. The laptops are used every day with an increasing number of requests from other groups to be included.

New learners are offered 'Computers for the Terrified' courses – giving those who have previously never touched a computer important initial contact. The sessions are supported by tutors who are there to work with the new users at their own pace and to offer much-needed encouragement and tuition.

The next stage is to offer those wishing to progress the opportunity to take the European Computer Driving Licence test supported with weekly sessions in the various communities.

WAKEFIELD BOROUGH COUNCIL ADULT EDUCATION SERVICE has a team of workers developing and co-ordinating community projects. The team consists of a Community Projects development officer, basic skills co-ordinator, outreach workers, tutors and a technician. Outreach workers identify groups/projects that want to use laptops. The development officer co-ordinates their use of the laptops and arranges for tutors. Up to three people may then go out with the laptops. In the longer term more outreach workers are being trained in ICT skills to be able to join the programme.

BARNSLEY COUNCIL, like other adult education services, was using laptops prior to the DfEE laptop initiative in order to offer FEFC-funded IT courses in the community. The DfEE laptops have enabled them to develop different types of work. Laptops have been given to tutors to work with specific target groups, e.g. travellers, people with learning disabilities in life skills groups, etc.

COMPUTER ASSISTED LEARNING AND TRAINING CENTRE
CALTEC is an off-shoot of Bradford LEA's Lifelong Learning provision. Its main role is to provide community education using ICT as a tool. There is a centre offering daytime ICT provision but a lot of the work is satellite provision: classes running in schools, community centres, and Asian women's centres.

CALTEC co-ordinated the use of the laptops and provided technical assistance. Community organisations were invited to apply to use the laptops and a plan for allocating their use was drawn up based on the response. Four projects were given use of them for an initial six months after which usage will be reviewed.

1. Cancer Support Centre – A high proportion of users are Asian women and the laptops enable the cancer sufferers to talk about their illness and their feelings;
2. Asian Women Mentoring Scheme – using the laptops to access training opportunities on the internet;
3. Youth Initiative – Producing Curriculum Vitae, application forms and accessing training and education opportunities;
4. A drug and alcohol project working on a one-to-one basis with recovering addicts in a church hall.

Laptop use is not so much about accessing vast amounts of people; it is more a long-term commitment to more disadvantaged groups – people who would not normally approach education of any kind.

NORTHAMPTON ADULT EDUCATION SERVICE has moved away from the idea of using the laptops directly with students, to using the laptops to support tutors' own ICT development. Tutors delivering return to work courses in rural areas were each loaned a computer in order to be able to:

- Communicate with other tutors using email;
- Develop learning materials and share with other tutors;
- Gain confidence in their use of ICT; and
- Use the laptop with the group of learners.

Tutors undertaking training on the City and Guilds 7306 programme were lent laptops; the aim being for them to be able to access the internet to develop resources to support their teaching.

Promotional events

- Laptops are a great tool for providing hands-on experience. Using CD ROM (e.g. IT for All, Computers Don't Bite, etc.) software that is easily accessible and fun, people can gain confidence in a relatively short time and feel they have achieved a positive outcome.
- Linking in with other events is an important part of outreach. By working with existing events you are not the only person doing the work and more often than not the focus is not on education and learning, but on having fun…so what better opportunity to slip learning in!

Town Mayor's Tea Party

Taking the Laptops to the Town Mayor's Tea Party on the International Day of Older Learners was the start of an 'Older and Bolder' project. The response was so overwhelming that a small grant was obtained in order to offer free daytime sessions to older learners in venues they identified. As a result of this project, computers have been obtained to leave in the venues and work is underway to develop older and bolder learning centres and a community website. (Oxfordshire)

Family Funday

"I saw in the local free paper that one of the local employers was planning a Family Funday. The advert was asking for anyone who was interested in setting up a stall. Stands promoting 'learning' are not very attractive when all you have to offer is a pile of leaflets. We had just got the laptops so we immediately saw this as an opportunity to take them out to the community. Our stall was under canvas next to the Bottle Stall and opposite the country and western music speaker. Using mostly CD ROMs we attracted and encouraged a large number of people who had never used a computer before to have a go. We also attracted a lot of children who brought their parents. As we didn't have games for the children they made way for the adults to have a go."

Learning points include:

- Laptops will run for a maximum of two and a half hours on batteries when using CD ROMs.
- It was important to have details of other provision available – not just computer courses.
- Whilst it was great to be next to the bottle stall the country and western music was a bit loud!

Taster sessions

Laptops and printers recently proved to be a useful device for attracting potential applicants to a coffee morning/enrolment session held in a church hall on an inner-city estate. The taster session included:

- Explanation of what courses are offered and what the learner can hope to achieve.
- Demonstration on how to use a mouse using a CD ROM Programme specially designed for beginners.
- Hands-on practice for those who wish to learn how to use the mouse.
- Tuition on what the 'Windows' system is and how to get into the Word programme.
- Using Word to create a poster using a large font and clipart.

Similar sessions could be set up using In-house/In-health, Webwise, Internet and scanners – targeting specific community groups. The secret is to take the laptops to where there is some kind of community activity already taking place. (Wakefield)

'We've been working with sheltered housing communities and use the laptops to see what interest there is. After which we encourage the housing associations who have IT training and money to work with the residents' associations to install PC's in the sheltered housing. A lot of people think older people don't want to know about computers!'

'We took the laptops along to a local Age Concern and showed it to the people who were over the moon. Basically they bought their own computer with internet connection, put it in what used to be the music room. It's on all the time now. Residents, day visitors, they can just come in and use it.'

Taster model

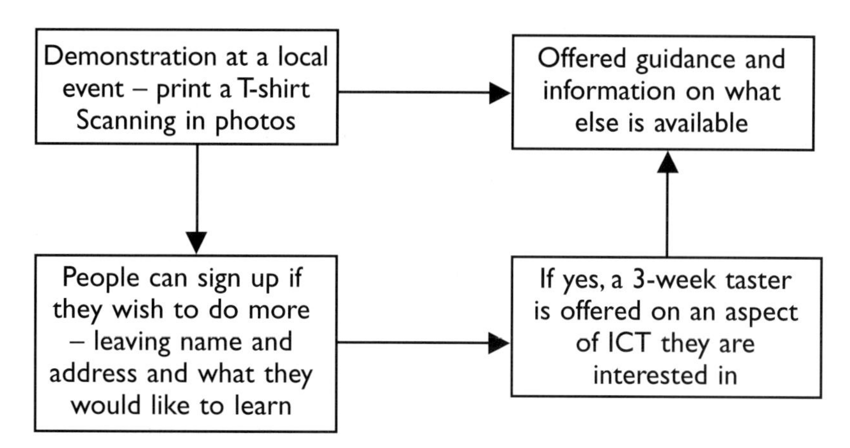

Supporting existing project work

There are many projects working within the community whose main focus may not be education, yet there is an incredible amount of learning going on. The use of portable ICT equipment has added value to this community work.

- Groundwork is an Environment Regeneration Charity using the environment to get people involved in their communities. The laptops are used in youth centres, schools, and drop-in centres – wherever the particular project is, and uses simple 3D Garden Design software.

Groundwork

'The way that I work, the community comes to us if they've got places near their houses they need doing up, or changing in some way. To actually catch the people that live round there, we have to actually go to them, they're not going to come to us. The computers have been really useful, to help explain how much time it actually takes to develop – if you've got a bit of green land, how much time it takes to develop it into a park or something – planning applications, things like that. We've got design packages, that help us to design it on the computers, so we don't just go and come back with a lovely picture. It actually helps them find out how much time it takes to develop, how much hassle is involved, just to decide how to do a path or something like that.' (Groundwork, Leeds)

Community Arts Project

The Forest of Dean Community Radio Programme has set up five community broadcast projects in the Forest of Dean since 1998. In that time a total of almost 400 hours of local material, created and produced by local people, have been broadcast. The introduction of laptops to this project through the DfEE Laptop Initiative has been welcomed. The laptops are used in a number of ways:

- typing up scripts;
- researching on the internet;
- as a resource to create news items; and
- as a research tool.

'I have been working with a group of mental health users who attend a day centre writing group. We are at the editing stage now so the laptop is really useful. At present I only have access to one. It would be great to borrow a few more.' (Community Arts, Forest of Dean)

Linking with others

Laptops are a valuable resource for contributing to partnerships. Here are some examples of how laptops can be used to enhance existing work:

- Networking with health visitors to offer a mothers and toddlers' group a basic computer course;
- A Health Centre and the local Youth Service are using the laptops in an initiative concerning the sexual health of young adults;
- A collaboration with Social Services has brought a scanner and a printer into use with a group of adults with learning disabilities;
- At the opening of a new advice and information centre the laptops, printers and scanners were used to digitise family photos;
- Laptops have been placed in libraries;
- As a result of taking the laptops into a working men's club, the club is now establishing a learning centre with a computer and library books; and
- The laptops have gone out with a local Information Bus.

Working with libraries

'As a county council we have a responsibility to empower our residents and IT is hitting everybody, whether they like it or not, whether it's getting money out of the hole in the wall, or whatever. One of the things that I'm doing with the laptops, is lending laptops out to libraries, because the libraries are developing and implementing an IT system. Instead of a paper-based system, people now have to use an IT catalogue. That is fine, but the majority of the people going into those libraries can't understand at the moment.

One of our responsibilities is to go into those libraries and give people basic IT tuition to enable them to use county facilities. Which may be nothing to do with education in tuitional terms, but more accessing information.' (Lancaster)

Technology at your fingertips

- A residential conference for people with learning disabilities provided an excellent opportunity to introduce technology. The aim was to produce a newsletter about the conference. The equipment consisted of 14 laptops, printers, scanners, digital camera, recording equipment, pens, paper, projector linked to a laptop, laminator and internet connection. Software included: Word, Publisher, Clipart, Wordsearch Construction Kit, Photo Express, Omnipage, In House and Powerpoint.

The delegates were encouraged to record their information by:

- Handwriting then scanning in;
- Handwriting then word processing;
- Taking photos using a digital camera;
- Word processing straight on to the laptop;
- Talking about experience to a support worker who wrote it down and then word processed it; and
- Listing words that could be fed into wordsearch construction kit
- Compiling the wordsearch and selecting the shape.

(Northampton)

Local history in the supermarket

Laptops, printers and scanners have been put to use by a voluntary organisation working with a local community school and Adult and Community Education service. Local residents are working on a local history project whose aim is to produce a community book.

The equipment was recently used in a story gathering session in a local supermarket. Having the scanners helped to create wider interest and draw more people into the project. People were asked to bring in photographs and stories. Some people brought photographs they knew little about and other people were then able to help piece together the history; individuals were encouraged to write or record their stories onto disc to be used in the book. (Wakefield)

Developing a project team

It takes time to do outreach development work with laptops.

It is therefore important that there is a team or a steering group to implement the laptop programme. Enthusiasm and commitment are crucial and clear understanding about what it takes to create a Learning Community. Assembling the right team might be the most important element of a successful laptop programme.

The team will need to oversee such rudimentary tasks as recording serial and asset numbers, determining electrical wiring needs, designing security procedures, processing the laptop orders, and organising laptop maintenance and repair. At the same time, the team must tackle such complex issues as:

- Allocation – developing systems for application;
- Prioritising – deciding who will have priority use;
- Thinking creatively and imaginatively about how to implement exit strategies where laptops have been used; and
- Fund-raising.

Ultimately, the success of your effort will depend on the talents, experience, personality, conviction, enthusiasm, and creativity of the people you involve. In selecting team members, keep in mind the vision statement that you have created and the learning goals you have defined.

The project leader

The first important issue surrounding the choice of a project leader, i.e. the person who will lead the team, is who makes the choice. The second issue is the qualifications that define a good leader. The project leader needs to have respect and influence in at least two areas: administration and instruction. Ideally, the leader should also have credentials in one or both of these areas. If necessary, consider appointing two people to lead jointly. This person may already be in post and will take on the role in addition to other duties.

Team members

The programme manager

Early on, you should assign one of your team members to be the programme manager. This person will oversee the entire programme for the next few years – from its beginning through to its growth into a mature programme. The programme manager should possess excellent programme management skills, including the ability to handle many details at one time. The programme manager will play many roles, such as:

- Co-ordinating, implementing, and reporting project milestones;
- Negotiating and co-ordinating with outreach workers, tutors, administrative staff and potential partners;
- Designing and implementing an internal support and diagnostics process for the laptops;
- Co-ordinating service arrangements for the laptops;
- Publishing progress reports and communicating with the project team;
- Facilitating staff training; and
- Developing presentations and informational material.

The outreach worker

Your project team will include outreach workers. Your outreach worker should be a person who:

- Adapts easily to new situations;
- Is creative;
- Is able to see the range of teaching and learning opportunities that laptops offer;
- Is a great team player;
- Believes strongly that laptops can play a powerful, creative role in curriculum development and delivery.

The outreach worker will facilitate the use of new technology within the community by identifying groups or individuals who would benefit from using laptops.

The roles of the outreach worker may include:

- Identifying groups;
- Identifying venues – assessing suitability;
- Promoting events;
- Working closely with tutors and technicians to ensure smooth operation; and
- Ensuring tutors employed are clear about aims and objectives of the project.

The support technician

A support technician is invaluable and needs to be identified as soon as possible.

The support technician's roles include:

- Providing first-line support and diagnosis of any problems that occur;
- Co-ordinating all repairs;
- Installing and advising on additional software;
- Overseeing maintenance, utility software such as virus protection, communications devices on laptops, and software upgrades;
- Maintaining an accurate registry of all equipment including full user details, serial numbers, insurance registration details and claims, and service profiles; and
- Providing a simple help desk for staff.

This is an ideal specification. For large organisations such as Local Education Authorities it may be possible to link the laptops programme into existing ICT system support. For smaller voluntary organisations you may need to consider using existing staff or volunteers from the community.

Technical support staff

You may need to employ support staff to accompany the laptops. In which case, their duties may include:

- Picking up the computers from a base;
- Taking them to a group;
- Setting them up;

- Remaining with the group throughout the session; and
- Returning the laptops to the base and reporting any technical difficulties.

ICT tutor

How you are using the laptops will determine the tutor you will employ. Using the laptops to widen participation and for basic skills, you will be looking for a tutor who:

- can support learners;
- has excellent communication skills;
- is sensitive to the needs of adult learners; and
- has a flexible approach.

This may provide an ideal specification. The experience of some people in taking possession of the DfEE laptops was that certain elements were not in place. It may have been that there was no money to provide for an infrastructure as described above. Where there was a need to offer ICT training to adults with basic skills requirements, there was a need to train basic skills tutors in ICT skills in the first instance.

Funding

If outreach work is to be truly effective it must be funded on a long-term basis. Short-term funding is very damaging to workers who need time to develop skills and to recipients who begin to develop relationships.

This laptop project has highlighted that, whilst there is no one formula of funding outreach and development work across the country, there has been significant growth in the recent years. This is due to specific funding opportunities such as:

- FEFC Widening Participation projects;
- Non-schedule 2 funding;
- Adult and Community Learning Fund;
- New Opportunities Fund – Community Access to Lifelong Learning;
- European Social Fund; and
- Single Regeneration Budget.

This is operating within a bidding culture where areas of disadvantage are the main recipients. Whilst it is true to say that outreach work takes time, so do applications to bid for funding.

EXTERNAL FUNDING BIDS

If outreach work is developing from the bottom-up then it takes time – time to identify needs and then work collectively with people in the community to meet the needs. Being able to meet that need might sometimes involve putting in bids to external funders.

It can take time to get things moving. The groups you are working with want instant results and the development time can be frustrating. If a bid is put into an external funder and is then unsuccessful, this can have disastrous effects.

> 'One thing is certain: tremendous damage can be done to people by getting them to stand on a rug only to pull it out

> from under them. A properly constructed outreach project must have an endgame strategy. The annual funding merry-go-round is not helpful in this context.'

'Mainstream institutions alone cannot make IT accessible for all. There are sound reasons for further funding for outreach development work.'

WORKING IN PARTNERSHIP

Other providers in the area where there is outreach work may be able to meet the needs arising. These might not necessarily be IT progression routes – there are all sorts of different ways learners can progress from basic IT. If a basic IT course has been offered, it is helpful to invite a representative from the college or a local guidance worker to talk to the learners and ensure they know what else is on offer and what funding there is for them to be able to do further learning.

'Funding for the computer courses we offer with the laptops comes from various sources. I'm trying to promote in the community self-financing groups. Groups are given information to apply for funding from different sources. I find that if a group finances itself it will almost certainly be more successful than a top-down project; it is their property. Of course not all groups will want to go for funding so then we can look to fund it via the college i.e. Partnerships.'

VALUE

This project has demonstrated what a tremendous difference having effective resources can make. It is not only valuing the people in the community but also the workers. Access to up-to-date resources is sending out a very important message:

"You are worth it ..."

'Up to two years ago, the only money available in adult community education was for basic skills. There was no other provision for adult education in the borough. That meant that if we were doing outreach, we were trying to get people into English and Maths groups, standing in car parks handing out leaflets!

Once we got laptops and were able to start with some computer classes it was easy to build bridges and now they're part of adult education funding. We've got funding from the LEA and it is part of a much wider link.'

Choosing software, hardware, peripherals, extras...

Organisations within the laptop initiative received a laptop package consisting of:

- Laptop – Pentium 300MHz, 32Mb Ram, 14" colour screen (in a carry case);
- Integral modem and access to the Internet;
- Lexmark colour inkjet printer (normal size);
- Cannon parallel scanner;
- MS Office Pro 97 (Word, Access, Excel, PowerPoint, etc);
- MS Publisher 98;
- MS Frontpage; and
- MS Encarta CD ROM

Experience has shown that you might wish to consider adding the following resources to your package:

- Additional Software – CD ROMS that encourage people to achieve IT for All, BBC Webwise, BBC Count Me In, BBC Computers Don't Bite, Games, Catalogues, Geoff Hamilton 3D Garden Design, In-House, In-Health, Driving Theory Test, and Guidance software;
- Laminator;
- Trolley to transport laptops – flat-bed fold-up trolley cost approx. £50–£80;
- Carry boxes to carry printer;
- Extension leads;
- External mice;
- Digital camera;
- LCD projector screen;
- Projector;

- Switch box for printers;
- Floppy discs; and
- Headphones.

LAPTOP COMPUTERS – BUYERS' GUIDE

The following guide provides information if you may wish to consider purchasing additional laptops and accessories

There is a wide range of laptops available with a bewildering range of options and specifications. However, do not allow the computer jargon to prevent you from accessing the suitability of the computer. Although we will use the term laptop, many suppliers call these types of computers notebooks.

The main objective is to buy equipment that will meet your needs and the needs of your students.

Simple Checks

If you are going to have to carry laptops, it is important to check how heavy the machines are. How easy is it for more than one learner to see the display and how clear is the display? Laptops have a number of different built-in devices to control the on-screen pointer (e.g. touch pad). New computer users often find these devices difficult to use so you should buy a separate mouse as many laptops will not be supplied with a mouse. You need to check that the mouse works with your machine. So try the laptop out, carry it about, view the display and check both floppy and CD-ROM drives. Sometimes the drives are supplied separate from the laptop and have to be plugged in. If this is the case, carefully check the drives. Are they likely to be damaged in use?

Virus Protection

It is essential that you obtain virus protection software and use it. If you do not install virus protection software then your laptop is likely to be infected. Viruses can be devastating so prevention is the only choice.

Internet

Most modern laptops were designed to incorporate a built-in modem and many are supplied with one in the form of a PCI card. Some suppliers are also offering free access to the Internet. However, check the conditions for using this service – often the help-line is costly to use with users being charged by the minute. Also check the cost of telephone calls to the Internet using this service. Is it more expensive than a local call?

It is also worth asking around to locate other users to find out how the service operates and in particular the speed of access and reliability of the connection.

Supplied Software

When you buy the laptop it will normally be supplied with software such as:

- Operating system (e.g. Windows 98)
- Word-processor, spreadsheet and database integrated system such as Microsoft Office, Microsoft Works, WordPerfect and Lotus Smartsuite.

Consider if the software is useful to you. It is only a useful extra if you are going to use it. Bundled software is often supplied without manuals so you are reliant on the software's help system to assist you learning to use the system. The key is to judge the quality of software in terms of its usefulness to you and not be carried away with the number of items included.

Maintenance and Warranty

The majority of suppliers will offer you some form of warranty at least for the first year and in many cases for three years or even longer. In many cases the service in year one is more comprehensive than in later years. Almost all suppliers require you to contact their maintenance helpline before they will accept that your computer needs repairing under the warranty. When you telephone the helpline you will be asked to carry out a series of tests and report them to the operator. This is to diagnose the problem and see if it can be rectified without sending an engineer out or returning the equipment. It can be a shock if you are new to computers to be asked to take the machine apart with a screwdriver but this can be requested by the helpline. If you are not prepared to follow the helpline's requests then they will often refuse to accept the machine can be repaired under the warranty. In many cases the fault can be rectified by following instructions from the helpline. If the problem is too difficult, then depending on the warranty, an engineer will be sent out or your equipment will be returned to the supplier for repair.

The two main warranty options are:

1. On-site maintenance – once you have agreed with the supplier (normally by telephoning the helpline) that your computer needs repairing, they will send an engineer to your location to repair it. This is normally the best option. However, it is worth reading the warranty carefully and asking how long the engineer will take to visit you.

2. Return to base – once you have agreed with the supplier (normally by telephoning the helpline) that your computer needs repairing, the computer is returned to the supplier for repair. In some cases the supplier will arrange for the equipment to be collected from you and in some cases it is your responsibility, so carefully check the warranty before you buy.

CHECKLIST FOR LAPTOP COMPUTERS

Processor type and speed	Pentium II 300 MMX (PII 300 MMX) or AMD K6 3 350 or AMD K6 2 333 or Celeron 300
Memory (RAM)	Minimum – 32MB Norm – 64MB Excellent – 96MB
Display Size	Minimum 12 inch
Display Type	TFT
Display Resolution	640 x 480 x 24 bit colour or better 800 x 600 x 24 bit colour or better
Video Memory	Minimum 2MB
Hard Drive Capacity	Minimum 3GB
Carrying Case	This is essential to protect your investment and is often not included in the standard price

Operating System	Windows 98
Weight with Batteries	Notebook
Battery Life	Minimum 90 minutes, more is very useful
Drive	Floppy and CD ROM drive ideally integrated but acceptable as separate plug-in devices
Modem	Internet modem essential
Mouse	Probably need but supplied in standard package
Virus protection software	Essential

Price is only one factor in buying a computer. You tend to get the specification you pay for. A good warranty is worth paying for so do not purchase solely on price.

Printers

There are now a wide range of printers available to you. Prices have fallen rapidly in recent years. In developing this package we have assumed that you would be buying an inkjet or low cost laser printer but you have the flexibility to adjust your purchase to meet your needs. Most printers are designed to be used in a fixed location so that if you plan to use them as a portable resource you should check if they are suitable. You may need to buy a carrying case or protection to ensure that the printers are not damaged. Suppliers often show you examples of the printer's output. However, these are usually printed on specialist paper specifically developed for that type of printer and costing several times more than the paper you are likely to use. They show the best output possible and when you print on your paper it will not be the same high quality.

Some simple items to check when buying a printer are:

Speed

This is usually expressed in how many pages per minute (ppm) can be printed. A standard (£140 to £350) inkjet printer should print at about 6 to 10 ppm (black text) and 3 to 5 ppm if they use colour. However, this usually depends on the resolution you have chosen. A high-resolution document (better quality) will print slower that a lower resolution one. Budget printers (less than £100) often print at rates of 3ppm (black text) and less than 1 ppm for colour.

Low-cost (£200 to £500) laser printers designed for the home or small office use are available but do not provide the option of colour. They offer speeds of between 8ppm and 10ppm.

Advertisements tend to quote the best possible speeds. So ask for a demonstration or buy a printer you have already used.

Resolution

Resolution is expressed in dots per inch (dpi) and the higher the resolution the better the quality of printing available. Printers can be set to a range of resolutions so you can choose the quality you want. Inkjet printers typically offer up to 600x600 dpi although some are capable of providing 1200x1200 dpi. However, in colour mode the resolution is reduced and is often half the black resolution (e.g. 300x300 dpi). Laser printers offer 600 to 1200 dpi. High resolution quality is normally at the expense of speed.

Inkjet and toner cartridges

Both inkjet and laser printers consume ink and toner respectively, so check how much a replacement cartridge costs when you buy a printer. In the case of inkjet printers there are two types: black and colour cartridges. If you print in full colour, you will be amazed at how often you need to replace the colour cartridge. Cartridges are specific to the model and type of printer. Inkjet cartridges typically cost between £15 and £30. Prices are considerably reduced if you buy in bulk. Laser toner cartridges are more expensive (e.g. £40 to £125) but tend to last longer. They are often supplied with a statement of capacity in terms of pages printed at a particular resolution (e.g. 5,000 to 10,000 pages).

Warranty

Printers also come with their own warranty which is usually limited to one year. As with computers, the options can be on-site maintenance or back to base. Check before you buy.

Scanners

The cost of scanners has fallen over the last few years so that budget machines can be purchased for under £100. In common with most parts of the computer market there is a wide choice of products available to you. The key factors you need to consider are:

Resolution

Resolution is measured in dots per inch (dpi) which the scanner will detect and appears fairly obvious. Unfortunately there are three different resolutions within a scanner. These are:

- Optical
- Mechanical
- Interpolated

Optical resolution is the key measure in that it is related to the light sensors if there are 300 sensors for each inch of the array then it has a resolution of 300 dpi. The number of sensors vertically and horizontally can be different so resolutions such as 300x600 dpi are possible.

Mechanical resolution relates to the number of steps the mechanical array makes per inch during the scan so if it makes 300 per inch it has a mechanical resolution of 300 dpi. It relates only to the vertical axis so horizontal resolution is usually the optical resolution. Flat bed scanners can normally achieve high mechanical resolutions.

Interpolated resolution is the highest resolution that the scanner is capable of achieving using software which fills in the gaps between the dots.

All this is logical but suppliers sometimes confuse the different types of resolutions. You need to ask but advertisements often quote optical and interpolated resolutions which are sufficient to decide on the scanner.

Budget priced scanners will often provide 600x300 to 600x1200 optical and 4800x4800 to 9600x9600 interpolated resolution while a medium priced machine (i.e. £100 to £300) offer 600x1200 to 600x2400 optical and 9600x9600 interpolated.

Colour depth

Colour depth is the number of shades of colour the scanner can distinguish between. This is expressed in bits and the more bits that a scanner can identify the better the quality of the image scanned. At the moment most scanners offer at least 30 bit colour although 36 and 42 bit colour is widely available. A 36 bit colour scanner can distinguish 68 billion colours.

Connection to the computer

There are a variety of ways of connecting the scanner to the computer. They are parallel port, USB port and SCSI.

- Many scanners simply plug into the parallel port of the computer. This is the same connection as the printer uses. It is possible to buy a cable which allows both the scanner and printer to work from the same parallel port.
- USB ports are relatively new so you need to check if the computer you are connecting to has the correct port.
- SCSI ports normally require a SCSI card to be installed inside the computer. This adds to the cost since SCSI scanners do not normally come with a card.

Software

The success of a scanner is dependent to a large extent on the software that you use. Most scanners are supplied with software. The main software to consider are:

- Twain compliant – most scanners come with Twain compliant software which allows any Twain compliant software application to have a scanning capability so you scan into a word-processing document or other application.
- Editing Software is the most obviously useful application in that images can be manipulated, enlarged, cropped and enhanced.
- OCR – Optical Character Reading software allows you to scan text into the computer and import it into a word-processing application.

Digital Cameras

There are many different digital cameras available to you. You need to decide what you need. The price of the majority of cameras is in the range £175 to £900 and there are many different models, specifications and suppliers in this range. The things you need to check are:

1. Most cameras provide you with a small LCD screen to preview the picture you have taken or aim to take. The bigger the screen the better, but in practice screens tend to be between 1.5 to 2.5 inches across the diagonal. Take a look at a few and decide what is best for you.
2. The controls of digital cameras can require some study to work out the different options so consider who will be using the

camera. If you want learners to be able to use the camera then probably you need one which has clear, easy-to-follow controls and instructions. It is worth reviewing the instruction manuals to see if they are suitable.

3. A key feature of a digital camera is capacity. How many pictures can the machine store? This is normally dependent on the size of the memory card supplied on which the pictures are stored. Many cameras allow you to remove memory cards and replace them with a blank card so capacity is dependent on the number of cards you have. Early cameras had a fixed store. The norm is now to employ memory cards.

4. Digital cameras are normally battery-powered, and a mains lead and converter is usually an extra. Check on how long the batteries will last. Some cameras are supplied with rechargeable batteries.

High Street or Mail Order

The two main sources of computers and accessories are retail outlets and mail order companies. The general advice is that you tend to get more for your money buying by mail order while it feels good to see who you are buying from when you go into a retailer. These are both stereotypes and the best advice is to compare prices, warranty and specifications before you go ahead. Some guidance for buying computers is given below:

1. Research the market by reading the magazines, visiting computer shops and discussing your needs with in-house or other neutral experts. Make a list of questions you want answered before you buy.

2. Ask your questions and make notes of the answers and record the name of the member of staff.

3. Check the warranty and maintenance offered – extended warranties are not often good value.

4. Confirm exactly what you will receive – sometimes the supplier reserves the right to offer a package of similar value if items are not available.

5. When the equipment is delivered or you take it away, ensure that everything is there and working. If you have a problem contact the supplier immediately or refuse to take it away.

6. Keep the packaging since this is very useful if you need to move the equipment or return it for repair.

7. Keep notes of all contacts with supplier including telephone calls and a file of all correspondence.

SOFTWARE AVAILABLE

BASIC SKILLS

New Reading Disc: This is a reading and writing program where all the text has been pre-recorded so students can hear the voice reading the text on the screen. There are six word games included and you can put on work of your own for specific students. They can, if they wish, record their own voice. This work is then also available for the games.

Words in Action: Similar to the Reading Disc but with a new range of topics.

Perfect Copy : This is a grammar and punctuation program (no voice) which is simple to use. Many students enjoy the challenge and are well motivated by the exercises. It can also be used for printing out worksheets.

Numbers Disc: This is a numeracy package covering the basics as well as fractions, decimals, percentages and so on. Again, there is sound so all text is read out if desired. The "Experience Exchange" and "Have Your Say" can provide good a discussion basis for literacy, ESOL as well as numeracy groups.

Numbers You Need: A series of five disks covering **Fractions, Decimals, Percentages, Negative Numbers and Approximation** and **Estimation.** Short programs, each of which can be worked through in 30–60 minutes by the student, with a few questions at the end.

Smile: this has 37 mathematical games, puzzles and investigations, which provide good experience for problem solving, a skill that employers increasingly value.

Theory Driving Test Disc: This includes all the questions from the test. There is voice for all the text and it can greatly improve reading skills as the student is motivated.

Licence to Drive: Concentrates on driving skills and know-how and complements the above.

An Eye for Spelling: This practises spelling word patterns and can help the very basic or dyslexic student. New patterns can be added.

GAMZ: Word card games and word searches, with emphasis on spelling patterns, particularly useful for poor spellers and those with dyslexia.

Wordshark: About 30 spelling and alphabet games with sound.

CV Generator: This gives three sample CVs as well as letters of application, with help on each section.

Form Filling: There are various formats with help and guidance at each stage.

SUBJECTS

In Health

Writing an Article
Access for All
May accidents never happen
Care
Feeling good, looking good
My Health
Parents know best
Look after the planet
Pregnancy and childbirth
Prevention is better than cure
Health at work

Having a Debate
AIDS, fact and fiction
Choose your poison
Complementary medicine
Ageing
Smoking

Writing a Letter
Tenants Association
Child's school
Editor of a local paper

In House

Writing an Article
Change – dependence to independence
How I feel
My ideal Home
Things I didn't learn at school
No home, no job
Owning a home
Knowledge is power
Keeping a roof over your head
Safety
The small print

Having a Debate
Choosing your home
Healthy living
Spending money
Active tenants
Us and them

Writing a Letter
Letter to the authority
Housing Benefit
Keeping in touch

Working with the media

It is great to see stories in the media that increase the visibility, status and accessibility of adult learning. Positive images of successful learners, descriptions of well-planned approaches, and inspiring ideas that could be adapted elsewhere will have a significant impact on practitioners, potential learners and policy makers. This persuades people of the value of imaginative, community-based learning.

PRESS

- Agree who within your organisation will deal with publicity and talk to the press;
- Use the newspapers, newsletters and specialist press in your area (geographically and thematically) and find out the type of stories they like. You don't need to restrict your approaches to the educational press or education correspondents;
- Make contact well in advance of your target date to discuss ways of getting coverage and invite them to attend an appropriate event or activity;
- Before you make your first approaches, assemble the materials you need. This could include facts and figures, photographs, examples of work (e.g. teaching and learning materials, CD-ROMs, web-sites, etc), an idea of things or places that would make good film or photographs, strong interviewees, anecdotes and learning stories. Decide upon the two/three key points you want to get across;
- Write a press release using lively and original 'human interest' stories and be clear about the basic facts (where, when, why and with whom). Be prepared to supply good photographs and to deal with further interest and enquiries; and
- Provide visiting journalists with full notes, including the names of those involved (with their permission) and a follow-up name and contact number.

RADIO AND TV

- Identify appropriate programmes (e.g. day-time chat shows, news broadcasts, special interest programmes, social action and community bulletins) and find out who deals with adult/ continuing education and community slots;
- Before you contact the producer, prepare a brief which covers your main points – editors and journalists are hooked (or not) by opening sentences. Good 'human interest' case studies are inspirational and effective copy. Be prepared to produce a punchy alternative if your first idea doesn't grab their attention;
- Arrange a meeting and supply the journalist in advance with a copy of your proposal together with background materials. At your meeting, discuss any extra support that may be needed to make the coverage more newsworthy. Check if the station has mechanisms for dealing with any resulting enquiries from viewers/ listeners; and
- Think about the way you would like the programme or interview to run. Are you prepared to broadcast live or would you rather have the piece pre-recorded? If you would prefer the former, agree the questions or broad topics in advance; if the latter, ask to hear a tape of the edited version before it goes out. In both cases, supply the journalist with full notes.

Remember...

Involve editors and journalists as early as possible and keep your contacts informed about your project as it develops.

- If you are taking or commissioning photographs, remember the most effective pictures show people *actively* engaged in learning. Cut out unnecessary background and focus upon the learners; and
- Always ask for and take note of deadlines. These are usually very short with radio, TV and newspapers. Magazines and newsletters may need the story several weeks prior to publication and women's magazines usually require several months' notice.

Evaluating outreach

Evaluation matters! All the way through the outreach work there is a need for evaluation. When initial goals are set at the start of a programme there is something to evaluate against. As you near the end of a development, it is crucial that you are able to evaluate the process to see that you have met your goals. A thoughtful evaluation process gives you feedback to build on for continued expansion and success.

How do you know what the benefits of community-based learning are? Do you measure it in terms of:

- More people engaged in life-long learning activities?
- More volunteers?
- An increase in partnerships?
- Greater networking?
- Development of learning organisations?

Whilst working creatively and innovatively in development work it is important to evaluate continuously; this allows lessons to be learned.

Who evaluates?

- Learners;
- Tutors;
- Outreach workers;
- Organisation; and
- Institution.

Keeping records and disseminating information

Within the laptop project there was no official record-keeping imposed on the organisations. However, records were kept and reports were written based on the organisations' record-keeping. NIACE conducted a research evaluation six months into the initiative. A questionnaire was sent to recipients of the initiative managed by NIACE. 100 organisations returned a completed questionnaire. The results of the questionnaire are summarised on the website at:

www.niace.org.uk/Research/ICT/laptops/results

One way of evaluating the benefits of outreach work is to look at where your programme fits in with the model below.

BENEFITS OF COMMUNITY-BASED LEARNING: OUTREACH WITH LAPTOPS

	Benefits	**Indicator**
Individual	Introduced to ICT Skills	Learning to learn
	Confidence	Engagement, volunteering
	Social skills	Communication, team working
Institutions	Organisation Development	Efficiency, involvement
	Collective asset base	Range of partnerships
	Learning organisation	Knowledge shared and used
Community	Capacity building	New skills
	Inclusion	New active members
Societal	Citizenship	Participation, responsibility
	Social Capital	Networks, values
	Social Identity	Physical appearance, pride

Based on Tavistock Institute/DfEE (1999)

Embedding/Conclusions

Some organisations had been using laptops prior to the DfEE initiative. These organisations already had systems in place and were able to expand and enhance the provision. For other organisations this was the start of a steep learning curve. The laptops arrived with no additional funding at a time when outreach and development work is not systematically funded within Lifelong Learning services. For those services that lacked the funding for outreach and development work, often the sole use of the laptops was for FEFC Schedule 2 funded courses.

The present push towards community development work from current initiatives such as this one has provided a forum for people to exchange information and look at examples of practice across the country.

The laptop initiative has:

- widened participation to many new learners, previously excluded from ICT services;
- broken down the fear of technology for thousands of new learners;
- acted as an invaluable tool for use in existing provision;
- provided the stimulus to create demand for ICT learning in new locations; and
- put outreach back on the map.

Within many organisations and communities new plans are being considered about using this resource to further develop 'Anywhere Anytime Learning'.

Main learning points from the use of laptops as an outreach tool are:

- Outreach work takes time and there is a cost;
- The laptops give a very clear message – *"You are worth investing in"*, both to people working in lifelong learning and the learners;

- Recruitment is not a problem when the laptops are on offer – *"they bite your hand off"*. Once systems and plans are in place this can be increased substantially.
- Drop out from laptop activity is virtually zero;
- Laptops offer greater flexibility in meeting the needs of learners. They do not all have to be doing the same thing;
- Laptops help to develop good group feeling, as they are not as imposing as PCs and this makes for a better learning environment;
- There are very real practical issues about transportation, collection and delivery, setting up in situ and the time that takes;
- Technical support is essential;
- Some people have concerns about the vulnerability of the machines and possibility of theft. A Health and Safety audit is necessary for the workers;
- Use of the internet was difficult in many outreach locations as phone lines were not easily accessible;
- As a result of the laptop work, many new partnerships have developed;
- Making-IT-Accessible, a mailgroup set up during this initiative, is invaluable in exchanging information about a wide range of matters;
- This initiative has highlighted a need for ICT training for workers engaged in lifelong learning.

References and further reading

Clarke, A (1999) *How to create effective information and communication learning programmes – a guide,* National Institute of Adult Continuing Education

DfEE (1998) *Demonstration Outreach Project: Identification of Best Practice Briefings – practical tips on individual themes.* Copies available Lisa Seymour, DfEE, IL3, Room E8d, Moorfoot, Sheffield, S1 4PQ

FEFC (1997) *Learning Works, Widening Participation in Further Education,* Further Education Funding Council, Coventry

Fordham, Poulton and Randle (1979) *Learning Networks in Adult Education*

Johnston, R (1988) *Outreach work – principles and policy.* Replan Issues

Replan Resources (1989) *Reaching out: Further Education and Work in and with the Community,* NIACE/REPLAN South/South West, Bristol

Ward, K (1986) *Replan Review 1,* Department for Education and Science

Ward, K (1988) *How to develop Outreach a practical guide.* Replan Issues

Appendix

Examples of systems developed to loan equipment

ADULT AND COMMUNITY LEARNING FUND – LAPTOPS INITIATIVE
PROJECT LOG

Centre name	*Project title*	*Contact name*	*Contact address*	*Tel/Fax Email*	*No. of machines loaned*

ADULT AND COMMUNITY LEARNING FUND – LAPTOPS INITIATIVE
PROJECT LOG

Start date	*End date*	*Centre name*	*Registration forms received*	*Loan agreement received*	*Final report received*

ADULT AND COMMUNITY LEARNING FUND – LAPTOPS INITIATIVE

INFORMATION SHEET

Project Title:

Organisation:

No of machines loaned:

You will now have collected your allocation of laptops in connection with the above initiative. It is essential that you complete and return the following documentation at the appropriate time. Please read this information sheet carefully:

1. **Loan Agreement** – 2 copies, both to be completed and signed and one returned to CALTEC.
2. **Participant Registration Forms** – 1 copy to be completed by each beneficiary on your project(s) and returned to CALTEC.
3. **Evaluation Questionnaire**.
4. **Evaluation Report**.

Loan Period

The initial loan period will be from week commencing 18 October 1999 until week commencing 18 February 2000, at which time all laptops will be returned to CALTEC. You will be eligible to apply for the second loan period along with any other projects who express an interest. Loan period extensions/amendments will be considered to fit in with specific project timescales.

Collection and delivery of Laptops

Your organisation will be responsible for collecting the laptops and associated equipment and software from CALTEC and for returning them upon completion of your project, together with any required paperwork.

Installation

Manuals are supplied with all hardware. Please consult these before setting up the laptops, printers and scanners. In particular, please ensure that the correct power adaptors are used for the scanner and printer, these are clearly labelled **as incorrect connection will result in damage to the hardware**.

Insurance

The insurance covers loss, damage and theft, provided this is notified to CALTEC as soon as possible after the incident and a record has been made in your Incident Book. Should you need to make a claim, please contact CALTEC in the first instance. The laptops are covered by Bradford LEA insurance in the following circumstances:

1. On the premises of an LEA training provider, under the terms of your project.
2. On the premises of a non LEA training provider, under the terms of your project.
3. On the premises of a school or college, under the terms of your project.
4. In a car owned by a staff member from any of the above, under the terms of your project. Please make sure that the equipment is out of sight and the vehicle is locked securely if to be left unattended.
5. In the home of a staff member from any of the above **(provided they have written approval from the project manager)**.

- The laptops are not covered by Bradford LEA in the home of a beneficiary of the project. You must arrange separate insurance for this eventuality. You must satisfy yourself with written evidence that this has been arranged.

Note – please advise us in writing what security arrangements will be made for the equipment whilst it is on your premises and where it will be located when not in use.

Maintenance of the Laptops

Your organisation and staff members/tutors will be responsible for setting up the laptops, and associated hardware and software and day to day maintenance, which includes replacing ink cartridges. Your staff will also be responsible for installing and uninstalling additional software which your project uses. A helpline number and on-line support is available with regard to technical matters such as Internet access and email, printer, scanner and software difficulties.

In addition there is a 12 month on site maintenance contract. In the event of a breakdown or malfunction of the equipment, please contact CALTEC who will arrange for an engineer to visit your organisation.

Telephone numbers to contact for technical support are:

Software queries:	G-CAT	–	01908 206300
Printer queries:	Lexmark	–	020 8280 1701
Scanner queries:	Canon	–	08705 143723

Consumables

Each machine will be supplied with a full colour and black/white ink cartridge at the commencement of the loan period. You will be responsible for replacing these should they run out during the loan period.

Internet Access and Email

Each laptop will have one year's free access to the Internet and the software for this facility has been pre-installed on each machine. The Internet Service Provider is U-Unet. You will need a separate password for each machine to access the Internet and these are attached.

You will be expected to join the electronic mailgroup called Making-IT-Accessible, which is intended to provide an electronic means for all participants to:

- Communicate and share experiences, ideas and problems
- Provide mutual support to each other
- Have access to experts, both within and outside of NIACE
- Have up to date information on developments such as the University for Industry, National Grid for Learning etc
- Ask questions and discuss issues

To subscribe to the group send an email to: Listcaster@niace.org.uk with the message: Subscribe Making-It-Accessible. Once you have joined the mailgroup, any messages should be addressed to: Making-It-Accessible@niace.org.uk. The mailgroup is intended for tutors and staff not students. When you have joined, please send a message explaining who you are and what you are planning to do with the laptops. If you have questions, comments, useful hints, resources to share, a relevant conference or seminar to advertise, send a message to the mailgroup to inform everyone else.

Microsoft Frontpage

The user name and password for this programme are as follows, please note they are case sensitive and should be typed in exactly as shown:

Log on: Administrator
Password: password

Saving beneficiaries' work

Anti-virus software has been installed on the laptops. CALTEC's Network Technician will upgrade this software on a regular basis. However, we recommend that participants are not encouraged to bring work in on floppy discs, to prevent the accidental introduction of a virus.

Monitoring and evaluation of the projects

You will be sent a questionnaire to complete approximately midway through the loan period of the project and this **must** be returned. Please note that a member of staff from CALTEC will visit each project at least once during the initial loan period and there may also be a visit from NIACE. In addition, CALTEC's Network Technician will visit at least once. You will be advised of the dates of any visits to your project.

As part of the loan agreement, you will be expected to provide an end of project Report to CALTEC with details of the project and how successful it has been, together with numbers of beneficiaries, venues, software used, whether your aims and objectives have been achieved and whether you wish to repeat the project over a further loan period.

If additional advice, information or support is required in connection with your project with regard to progression for participants, or additional training required, please contact CALTEC.

Also attached is a copy of the Project log, containing details of the other participants in the initial loan period. If you would find it helpful to network with each other during your projects, please do so.

ADULT AND COMMUNITY LEARNING FUND – LAPTOPS INITIATIVE

LOAN AGREEMENT

Centre:

Project Title:

Start Date:

End Date:

Loaned equipment:

Details	*Quantity*	*Reference number*	*Location of Laptops (please complete)*	*Checked in by (office use only)*

Declaration:

The above equipment is loaned on the basis that it:

- will only be used for the project specified and according to the information sheet provided
- will be kept in a safe and secure location
- will be returned in the same condition as when it was loaned
- will be returned by the due date

Signed: ....

Name: ....

Position: ....

Date: ....

LAP TOP PROJECT
COMMUNITY EDUCATION

EVALUATION

Project: *Date(s):* *Tutor(s):*

NIACE, who have provided the laptops, are required to provide an evaluation of the laptop initiative to the Department of Education and Employment. It would be really helpful if you could find a few moments to answer the questions below.

Please describe briefly how the laptops were used. Including what programs you used i.e. Publisher, Internet, Websise.

How many people participated in the course/activity?

Have you any learning points to share?

Is there anything else you would like to say about the laptops?

Signed: Date:

Return to:

OXFORDSHIRE COUNTY COUNCIL
Community Education
LEARNING FOR LIFE